Contents

Written by
Dennis Hamley

Illustrated by
Mark Boardman

Series editor **Dee Reid**

Heinemann

Part of Pearson

Characters

Dan

Jade

Tricky words

- nervous
- carriage
- flickering
- answer

- emergency
- squealed
- destroyed
- disappeared

Read these words to the student.
Help them with these words when they appear in the text.

Introduction

Dan had been for a trial at a football club in London. He had been really nervous and the trial hadn't gone well. It was dark and stormy as Dan got on the train to come home. He had a feeling something terrible was going to happen. Someone sat down beside him. It was his sister Jade. How did she get there?

The Last Journey

Dan had a trial at a football club in London. He was really nervous.

"What's up with you?" said his sister, Jade. "I thought you wanted to go for this trial?"

"I do," said Dan, "but I keep thinking something terrible is going to happen."

"Well, you know I'm always there for you," said Jade as Dan left for the train.

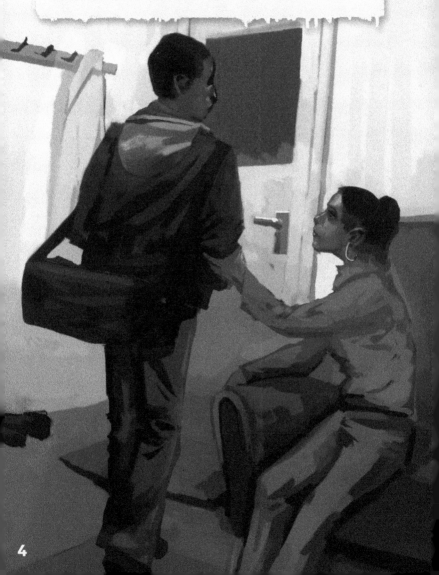

The football trial didn't go well.
Dan was fed up.
He knew he hadn't played well.
He just wanted to get home.

Dan got on the train.
The carriage was nearly empty.
Dan sat by the window and looked out.
It was pouring with rain.

The storm got worse.
The rain lashed against the windows.
The wind made the carriage rock
from side to side.
The lights in the carriage kept flickering.

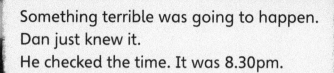

Something terrible was going to happen.
Dan just knew it.
He checked the time. It was 8.30pm.

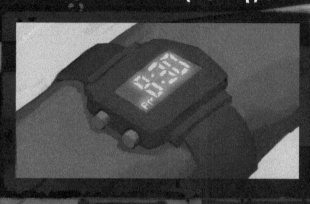

Someone sat down beside him.
It was Jade.
Dan was amazed.
"How did you get here?" he asked.
Jade didn't answer.

"Are you OK? You look ill," said Dan.
"You must stop the train," said Jade.
"I can't do that!" said Dan.
"Then I will," said Jade.

There was an emergency handle by the door.
Jade reached up and pulled it down.
Dan grabbed her hand to try and stop her.
Jade's hand was cold. So cold that he
let go of it. The brakes squealed.
The train came to a stop.
"What have you done?" cried Dan.

EMERGENCY
BRAKE

Jade opened the train door.
"What is going on?" asked Dan.
"Come with me," she said.
They climbed out of the train.
"This way," said Jade.

They walked along the track.
Jade stopped by the edge of a river.
"Where's the bridge?" said Dan.
"It's gone," said Jade.

The train had stopped right at the edge of the river.
The rails ahead were broken.
The bridge had been destroyed.

Dan looked down at the river.
"If you hadn't stopped the train it
would have crashed down into the river.
We would all have been killed,"
he said. "How did you know?"

Jade didn't answer.
Dan turned to look at her.
She had disappeared.

Dan looked all around for Jade,
but he couldn't see her.
Then the police arrived.
Dan got on a bus which was
taking people to safety.
"Jade must be on another bus,"
he thought.

Dan's mobile rang. It was his mum.
"Oh, Dan," she cried. "There's been a terrible accident. Jade's dead."
"She can't be," said Dan, "I've just seen her."

"She was knocked down by a car. The driver didn't stop," cried his mum.
"What time was it?" asked Dan.
"8.30pm," said his mum.

"But Jade was on the train with me then,"
said Dan. "She saved my life."
Then he remembered what Jade said
before he left for his football trial:
"I'm always there for you."
Dan put his head in his hands and cried.
If only he could have been there for Jade ...

Quiz

Text comprehension

Literal comprehension
p3 Why was Dan going to London?
p13 How did Jade save Dan's life?

Inferential comprehension
p7 Why is it important that Dan checked the time?
p7–8 What were the clues that Jade was a ghost?
p8 Why wouldn't Dan pull the emergency handle?

Personal response
- Do you like ghost stories?
- Where do you think Jade has gone?

Word knowledge

p6 Find a word that means going on and off.
p9 Find two powerful verbs.
p15 Find a word that means dreadful.

Spelling challenge

Read these words:

many   something   around

Now try to spell them!

Ha! Ha! Ha!

What sports are trains good at?

Track events!

Find out about

- some terrible bridge disasters around the world.

Tricky words

- useful
- journeys
- built
- collapse
- knocked
- disasters
- pillars
- Mississippi River

Read these words to the student. Help them with these words when they appear in the text.

Introduction

Bridges are very useful. Journeys would be much longer if trains and cars couldn't cross rivers. Most bridges are very safe and last for hundreds of years. But sometimes things go wrong and bridges collapse. There have been bridge disasters in America and a terrible bridge disaster in Scotland.

Bridges

Bridges are very useful.
If we didn't have bridges,
people would find it harder
to cross busy roads.
Trains and cars wouldn't
be able to cross rivers and
journeys would be much
longer.

Most bridges are very safe.
They are made by experts.
Some bridges are so strong that they have
lasted for hundreds of years.
This bridge in Italy was built in 1345 and it is
still used today!

But sometimes, things go wrong and
bridges collapse.
Some bridges have been knocked down
by floods. Some bridges have been knocked
down by strong winds. Some bridges
just weren't built very well
and they collapsed.

Bridge disasters

In America in 1861, some outlaws attacked the bridge over the River Platte. They set fire to the wooden pillars holding up the bridge.
The bridge looked as if it was OK. But it wasn't!
The bridge was very weak. When a train went over it, the bridge collapsed and the train crashed into the river. 20 people were killed and over 100 were badly hurt.

There was another bridge disaster in
America in 1876.
It was a freezing cold day and a train was
pushing its way through deep snow.
It started to cross the bridge over a river
but the train and the snow were far too
heavy for the bridge and it collapsed.
The train crashed into the river.
Over 90 people were killed.
Later it was found that the bridge
had not been well made because
the builders were trying to save money.

There was a terrible bridge disaster in Scotland in 1879 when the bridge over the River Tay collapsed.

The Tay Bridge was nearly 3 miles long and people thought it was wonderful. Queen Victoria even came to open the bridge. But it turned out that the bridge had not been well made.

One night there was a storm.
The wind was very strong.
A train was crossing the Tay Bridge
on its way to Dundee.
People waiting at Dundee station
could see the lights of the train as
it began to cross the bridge.
Suddenly the lights of the train
went out.

The bridge had collapsed and the train crashed into the river.
All 75 people on board were killed.
Only 46 bodies were ever found.

Modern-day bridge disasters

Not all bridge disasters happened a long time ago. There was a big bridge collapse in America in 2007.

The bridge was an 8-lane motorway over the Mississippi River. Thousands of cars, trucks and buses crossed the bridge every day.

One day the bridge suddenly collapsed. There were over 100 cars, trucks and buses on the bridge at the time. Lots of them crashed into the river below.

A school bus carrying 60 students was on the bridge when it collapsed.

Luckily, all 60 students were rescued.
Other people were not so lucky.
13 people were killed and 145 people
were hurt.
Later they found that the bridge
hadn't been built very well.
A new bridge which was much safer
was built in its place.

Don't panic!

Most modern-day bridges are very safe. There is very little chance that they will collapse. So don't panic next time you cross a bridge!

Quiz

Text comprehension

Literal comprehension
p22 Why did the bridge over the River Platte collapse?
p29 Why did the bridge over the Mississippi River collapse?

Inferential comprehension
p19 What did people do before there were bridges?
p23 Why might some bridges not be well made?
p31 Why might some people panic when they cross a bridge?

Personal response
- How do you think the people at Dundee station felt when the train lights disappeared?
- Would you be nervous crossing a very high or wide bridge?

Word knowledge

p20 Why is there an exclamation mark after the word 'today'?
p23 Find an adjective to describe the snow.
p29 Find a word that means 'injured'.

Spelling challenge

Read these words:

below   built   used

Now try to spell them!

Ha! Ha! Ha!

Why did the orange stop on the bridge?

Because it ran out of juice!